Musician Warrior King

JOHANNES AMRITZER

MUSICIAN WARRIOR KING

THE LEADERSHIP DNA OF KING DAVID

Original version published in Swedish by Paulus Media AB, Arlandastad, Sweden,
with the title Musiker Krigare Kung
Copyright © 2007 Johannes Amritzer

English copyright © 2009 Paulus Media AB
Translation: Nancy Eurell
Cover: Rickard Widell
Design. Samuel Willkander
Illustrated by Gary A. Smith

Distributed by Paulus Media in cooperation with Mission SOS
Printed by Raff Printing Inc. (USA) 2009
ISBN: 978-91-977193-3-9

Contents

Dedication

I would like to dedicate this book to Peter and Martina Almqvist who lead and direct our Mission SOS office in the United States of America. Martina has been Johannes' secretary for ten years and is also the Director of our international office. Peter has worked with us since 2000. He has been and continues to be our festival coordinator and manager since 2002. The Almqvists have whole-heartedly and sacrificially served in the work of the Holy Spirit through Mission SOS, and have been a blessing to us personally. They have given their lives, the majority of their time, all of their gifts, talents and money for the spreading of the Gospel. They live, breathe, dream, pray and speak nothing other than missions to unreached people groups. Peter and Martina are the pillars of Mission SOS' faithful team of workers. They are true leaders and fantastic workers! They are like our own family members that we have received through Jesus' blood covenant and we stand together in this work birthed by the Holy Spirit. Peter and Martina, we love you more than you could ever fathom!

Sincerely yours forever,

Maria and Johannes Amritzer

Foreword

In a time when the term leadership has been devalued, I gladly welcome a book that is about more than just the right strategies and visions. I believe in a new generation of leaders with integrity, character and high standards, leaders that are not afraid to get their hands dirty, work hard or to get a little criticism.

Johannes Amritzer has more than enough credibility and experience to write a book about leadership. I have personally seen him off stage. We have cast out evil spirits together during festivals around the world, hunted moose in northern Sweden, prayed for the sick and preached the gospel in the most incredible places. We have laughed, cried and even sweat together. I am an eyewitness of the fact that Johannes is a capable and competent leader whether he is on or off of the platform.

The principles for leadership taken from the life of King David are just as relevant today as they were when David conquered Goliath on the battlefield. Johannes has been able to grasp these principles coupled with his own experiences. He is able to express in this book a form of leadership that is greatly needed in many Christian circles.

A leader is one who cannot help but lead, guide and change. This book will help you to be stronger, more efficient and excellent in all that you do.

I myself, am a result of the type of leadership that is presented in this book, I am both a bond slave and one who was born on the battlefield. Together with Johannes I have been able to form and fashion many new leaders for the Kingdom of God.

I hope that Musician, Warrior, King will be a guide for the young generation of leaders that is being raised up to win the world for Jesus Christ!

Per Gisselsson
Field Director Mission SOS, Asia

Foreword by Author

The book you are holding in your hand is written as a tribute to our leaders at Mission SOS. This book is also directed to other leaders who like us have committed their lives for the sake of spreading the Gospel and the expansion of the kingdom of God to all unreached people groups. Many of the examples are personal and gained from our own experiences. This is done purposely in order to shed light on leaderships' many different aspects. The book is written as an encouraging guide for all of our own heroes, but will also most assuredly give many thoughts and ideas for those who are not working within Mission SOS. The teaching is not directed solely for pastors and missionaries, but is much broader and can be used for all types of leadership such as the business community or world of sports.

For understandable reasons, however, the focus of this book is towards church planters. The teaching focuses more on the principles of leadership and character than on leadership structures, visions and objectives.

Musician, Warrior, King, uses the Bible, focusing mainly on King David's life and leadership as a foundation for a teaching that is born, tried and tested in our work in northern

Stockholm as well as our missions work among the unreached people groups. David's life is fascinating and well worth a deeper study than what I am covering in this short book. I make no claims of being comprehensive when it comes to David's life and leadership.

This is, as other things in life, just the beginning of a journey and a Bible study that most surely will result in an eventual continuation of the subject later on. I pray for you, the reader. I have prayed that you would not get stuck on the small details that you may or may not agree with, but that you would rather receive the sum of the book's teaching as a whole. I read the Bible and see things from my perspective and you with yours. What we all need to do is to train ourselves to put aside our denominational spectacles and sort out the parts that are simply religious tradition and let the Bible speak to us.

This teaching is naturally tainted by my experiences and my journey through life. Some of the leadership principles in this book I have lived and practiced for many years, while others I still struggle with trying to live up to. I am not perfect, so please have patience with me. Let your heart be blessed and enriched. God bless you!

For the sake of the unreached peoples,

Johannes Amritzer
President of Evangelical Mission SOS International

A leader can be either man or woman, but for simplicities sake I have chosen to describe a leader in this book as he. There is no other underlying significance other than making the text easier for the reader.

Chapter 1

THE IMPORTANCE OF LEADERSHIP

A leader is important. A true leader is one who sees clearly and plainly the path ahead and above all, farther than the average person. A true leader stands out in the crowd and is a step ahead. That is why we call a leader a leader, because he has the ability to lead others. A true leader never needs to say obey me, rather he just simply leads and others follow him. A true leader thinks bigger than those who he or she is to lead. He goes before and paves the way with his life as an example. He is goal oriented, disciplined and constantly moving forward. He usually has a broader and higher perspective on things and does not compromise with his moral or ethical code.

A true leader possesses a large degree of courage to stand up for his beliefs and does not fall prey to peer pressure or the influences of the crowd. A true leader is a trend setter and has a vision in life that is greater than his own career and success. He lives and leads with the conviction of doing what is best for others. A true leader washes the feet of those he leads in a continual giving of himself. A spiritual leader has also heard the voice of God speak and has received His grace, strength and ability to lead, which makes all the difference. A spiritual leader is driven by a heavenly vision and has received a mandate from God. It is not a bad or shameful thing to be a leader and dare to lead. It is important that leadership is encouraged and appreciated, especially leadership that is unselfish and authentic.

When King David, the country of Israel's greatest and most talked about king, was at the height of his career his son Absalom rebelled against him. The young and handsome prince started to manipulate and seek the favor of the people to his advantage. Absalom's plot and conspiracy grew and grew until a full scaled revolt was a reality.

> "...and so he (Absalom) stole the hearts of the men of Israel."
>
> **2 Samuel 15:6b**

David, who had the experience, muscle, organization and finely tuned military machine, delayed action in retaliating against his own son. What kind of father would not have done that?

First David fled from Jerusalem and took the blasphemy and verbal abuse from his own people. When confrontation with his son was inevitable and finally took place, the whole future of the kingdom was at risk, so David enlisted soldiers. Commanding officers were appointed and the most experienced warriors in the king's army, Joab, Abishai and Ittaj lead the troops into battle to snuff out and extinguish the revolt. Then in keeping with his character King David said, *"I myself will surely march out with you."* 2 Samuel 18:2b.

That was why King David was so loved by his people. He was one of them and did not draw back in exclusivity when danger threatened the whole kingdom's safety. Rather, he willingly bore arms and placed himself on the frontlines of battle. The response of the people clearly showed the greatness and importance of the king's leadership:

> *"But then the men said, "You must not go out; if we are forced to flee, they won't care about us. Even if half of us die, they won't care; but you are worth ten thousand of us."*
>
> **2 Samuel 18:3**

Wow, what words! King David was worth as much as ten thousand men? Was that really true? Yes, I believe so. A great, notorious and experienced leader is much more valuable in both the peoples and God's eyes. No one person is ever irreplaceable, but the role of a leader should definitely be upgraded and appreciated more than we usually do.

When the Apostle Paul taught and instructed his spiritual son Timothy on how one leads a New Testament church, he said this about leadership:

"The elders who direct the affairs of the church well are worthy of double honor, especially those whose work is preaching and teaching."

I Timothy 5:17

Paul was saying here that a leader who managed his task well was worth double honor. What does double honor mean? Twice as much appreciation, respect and a higher salary than those he leads. Why? Because he is so vital. A leader needs your support, help, appreciation, but most of all, your respect. Without the leader your success would not be possible. The leader actually creates the spiritual and physical conditions for you to be able to develop, grow, blossom and bloom. To properly appreciate, value and show respect for your leaders is very pleasing to God and is rewarded directly from heaven. The Apostle Paul taught and said:

"I urge, then first of all, that requests, prayers, intercession and thanksgiving be made for everyone - for kings and all those in authority...this is good, and pleases God our Savior..."

I Timothy 2:1-2a, 3a

Pray for your leaders! Bless your leaders! They need your care, prayers and blessings. Honor and appreciate them!

*"Give everyone what you owe him: If you owe taxes,
pay taxes; if revenue, then revenue; if respect, then
respect; if honor, then honor."*

Romans 13:7

Paul said to the Christians in Rome that it was their obligation to show respect and honor to leaders. Obligation
is a strong word and perhaps a word not so popular in in-
dividualistic Europe or America, especially in reference to
honoring leaders. Duty and obligation towards leaders is
biblical and will result in a flood of blessings for him who
dares to believe and practice the Word.

*"Everyone must submit himself to the governing
authorities."*

Romans 13:1a

Everyone, including leaders need to be under authority.
I myself am under authority as in national and international spiritual mentorship. I have spiritual fathers who I
have submitted and entrusted myself to. Two in particu-
lar are Curt Johansson, leader of Trosgnistans Mission and
Ron Johnson, who leads an international apostolic network
ICAN. International Coalition Apostolic Network. It is a
fantastic blessing for me.

Be practical in showing love to your leaders. Release
them and help them to be able to devote their time to that
which they actually should do *"...prayer and the ministry
of the Word"* Acts 6:4b. Maybe you can give them a much

needed vacation or offer them practical, everyday help such as helping them grocery shop, do the laundry, clean, change tires on the car or wash the car. Treat them to something special now and then, surprise them!

Maria and I have put this into practice for quite a few years now and God loves things like this. He just pours back blessings over our lives when we show our appreciation for our leaders. To keep our eyes peeled, looking out for a leader around us who seems tired and in need of encouragement has almost become a fun and challenging sport for us. We have also received much of the same kind of appreciation and love from our beloved co-workers and those whom we lead. What a glorious and heavenly atmosphere it becomes when a congregation and an organization puts honoring and respecting its leaders into practice!

A few years ago when Maria and I really needed rest and relaxation during a very hectic time, the Almqvist family bought us a trip to Gotland, Sweden. It meant so much to us at that point in time. The care in which this gesture showed meant more to us than the trip itself with its cozy cottage. The care they showed created the warm feeling that we were appreciated. We were able to carry that with us for a long time.

Recently, I was given a night at a nice hotel in Stockholm. This was a wonderful surprise present from the young family of Jonatan and Anna Kvist. They lead our dance and evangelization work in Mission SOS and SOS Missions Bible College.It was a romantic evening for my wife and me, with a nice dinner at a restaurant, a movie and a chance to sleep in the next morning while Jonatan and Anna watched our two kids. Those 24 hours came after a time of intensely hard work and we were extremely tired when we left, but after 24 hours our batteries were recharged and we felt rested and ready to take on the Great Commission again. This is just the kind of expressions of love from our co-workers and our Christian brothers and sisters that make it so we have the strength to continue to fight the good fight for the sake of the Gospel.

Ever since I was a boy I have had a passion for hunting, fishing and adventure in the outdoors. Anders Landström, outside of Storuman in Lappland, northern Sweden understood this. He invited my father Ewald, a co-worker Per Gisselsson and me on an unforgettable hunting adventure in the Swedish wild. On October 22, 2002 I got to shoot a large moose with seventeen point antlers, a fantastic trophy! I will never forget this great hunter Anders and his wife Lovisa's generosity, hospitality and kindness those days up in Lappland. I thoroughly enjoyed life with a capital L. A photograph of me squatting down with my hunting rifle in hand, next to a huge moose was in the middle of my Bible for at least a year afterwards!

Now, you probably think I am crazy, but it meant so much to me. My wife had to finally tell me to shape up and stop carrying around that old torn photograph of the bloody moose and showing it to everyone I met. I told the hunting story to everyone everywhere I went and even mentioned it in my sermons sometimes. I wanted to include this in my teaching about leadership because it is just this kind of care and experiences that gives a leader strength to continue to preach the gospel with power without burning himself out.

By the way, God's Spirit does not burn anyone out, but the devil definitely has a break the leader down agenda! You can be part of undermining Satan's attacks on your leadership by serving your leader. Leadership is so important and you as a leader should hold your head up high. Good days are coming to Europe and America and strong leadership is rising up with a lions roar!

CHAPTER 2

QUALITIES OF A LEADER

Not everyone is a natural leader. Not everyone can be a leader. Some lead and others follow. Approximately 10 percent of humanity has leadership qualities. It is trendy and popular to say today that anyone can be a leader, but it is not true and only creates an unnecessary frustration for those who try to be something that they really are not. It is relief and freedom to finally realize where you are and where you are not gifted. Either you are a leader with leadership qualities or you can allow yourself to be led and be happy and satisfied with that. The sooner you realize who you are and your capabilities, the sooner you can actually begin to live and enjoy this life God has given.

Frustration, stomach ulcers, sleeplessness and stress are not the signs of leadership abilities and spiritual leadership. Constant anxiety over being unable to measure up is a clear sign and indication that you are in the wrong place in life and need to make an immediate change. Naturally, a leader sometimes goes through rough patches, and has to make difficult and unpopular decisions. A leader sometimes has to take a lot of criticism and misunderstanding, but when it comes down to it, he still enjoys his role as a leader.

A leader has a natural born gift and ability from God to lead. You have most likely heard the expression, born leader; good expression!

During the reign of Israel's first king, King Saul's government, there was a saying about a young shepherd boy named David:

> *"One of the servants answered, I have seen a son of*
> *Jesse of Bethlehem who knows how to play the harp.*
> *He is a brave man and a warrior. He speaks well and*
> *is a fine-looking man. And the Lord is with him."*
>
> **1 Samuel 16:18**

Even when David was just a young teenager, one of King Saul's servants recognized the leadership capabilities and talents of this shepherd boy. Everything was already there in his teen years, it just needed to be sharpened, polished and developed before David could step forward and become Israel's greatest and most notorious king in history.

David had leadership qualities and gifts that were apparent to everyone:

1. A skilled musician
2. A brave and mighty warrior
3. A gifted speaker

4. Good looks
5. The Lord was with him

The first three qualities in David were gifts and talents which can be developed and sharpened. Being good looking is a little more difficult, and in this book, I'm not going to encourage anyone to get plastic surgery! However, looking good is not completely unimportant for a leader, even though it may seem strange when first considered in this text.

A leader who only has great talent will not be taken seriously if he is not sensitive to different kinds of contexts, cultures and interactions with different kinds of people. You don't necessarily have to look like a model, be a body builder or be super trendy and cool to succeed, but dressing for the occasion, hairstyle, good hygiene and good manners are important.

The fact that the Lord is with you makes all the difference in being a spiritual leader than just an ordinary leader. The balance between anointing or spiritual presence, as well as talents or gifting is especially important for those who are blessed with many gifts and talents. Give your gifts back to God. Let Him anoint them. Sanctify and dedicate yourself to God. Let His Spirit show you how to succeed as a leader and most of all, how you should lead.

"Commit to the Lord whatever you do, and your plans will succeed."

Proverbs 16:3

"It was he who gave some to be apostles, some to be prophets, some to be evangelists and some to be pastors and teachers, to prepare God's people for works of service, so that the body of Christ may be built up"

Ephesians 4:11-12

It says, It was he who gave. Leaders are gifts from God to mankind as spiritual leaders are to the body of Christ.

"We have different gifts, according to the grace given us...if it is leadership, let him govern diligently..."

Romans 12:6a, 8b

According to the apostle Paul, the ability to lead is a gift from God. *"Leadership...to govern"* (1 Cor. 12:28b). God is the one who gives the gift or ability to lead.

God gives the basic equipment to every person, a toolbox full of gifts, talents and abilities. Not everyone has the same qualifications, but everyone has certain qualifications. A potential leader needs to be trained, exercised and developed. A leader needs to build strong leadership muscles and obtain experience by actually leading.

Because a leader is to lead, he learns while he is leading. It is impossible to hinder someone with leadership qualities from leading. The ability to lead is a quality that lies deep in the nature of the leader just as the ability to hunt lies in a young lion. The young lion learns from the older, more experienced lions how to be a better hunter while he is in the process of hunting.

Sometimes experience comes at a high price and tough lessons are all part of life's school of hard knocks. Those experiences, however, are priceless and invaluable for a leader who is constantly growing and developing. Some leaders have greater potential than others and in time may even become a leader of leaders.

When other leaders discover a potential leader, they can acknowledge this person and give their approval. They can appoint this person to the leadership roll he is already functioning in. Titles and clear duties and tasks are important because they provide the leader a security in functioning in his leadership.

The apostle Paul was not afraid to have a title. When we read the introductions to all of his epistles in the New Testament, we discover how bold and secure he was in his roll as a leader. That is why the installation and dedication of a leader is very important and should not be despised. The title and roll is not a medal on his chest, but should instead be seen as a clear job description. If there were not titles like carpenter, plumber, electrician at a construction site, there would be complete chaos, with nothing really being accomplished.

In order for God's house to be properly built it is necessary to have the spiritual roles and job descriptions specified. We need to know who is supposed to be doing what. Isn't it strange that it is okay to have the title evangelist or teacher in Sweden, but not apostle or prophet? Okay, now I have said it. To exaggerate or have excessive titling is not good either. The fruit always confirms the kind of tree we are dealing with. An apple tree bears forth apples and a plum tree brings forth plums. An evangelist leads people to faith in Jesus Christ. An apostle plants churches.

True spiritual leadership is not guided by democracy's societies or the business world's standards and rules. Not everyone is to lead, therefore, the majority should not decide who should lead, but leaders should choose leaders. Spiritual leadership is comparable to parents in a family where children don't get to decide who their parents are.

If my wife Maria became a widow and chose to remarry, she would very carefully choose who would be the children's new father. She wouldn't let the children vote on it. As a parent one has more insight, sees farther and understands better which qualities are the most important for the new dad to have. A leader is a leader for just that very reason. Otherwise the roll of a leader would be totally unnecessary. Spiritual leadership is also chosen in cooperation with the Holy Spirit. This is what the New Testament says about leadership in the church of Antioch:

> "While they were worshiping the Lord and fasting,
> the Holy Spirit said, "Set apart for me Barnabas and
> Saul for the work to which I have called them. So
> after they had fasted and prayed, they placed their
> hands on them and sent them off."
>
> **Acts 13:2-3**

It also says about the chosen leaders Barnabas and Saul:

*"Paul and Barnabas appointed elders for them in
each church and, with prayer and fasting committed
them to the Lord."*

Acts 14:23

Leaders are to appoint and choose other leaders. The apostle Paul says to one of his spiritual sons Titus:

*"The reason I left you in Crete was that you might
straighten out what was left unfinished and appoint
elders in every town, as I directed you."*

Titus 1:5

During the first few hundred years of the New Testament Church there was not a trace of democracy when it came to identifying, dedicating and appointing leaders. The apostles and the pioneers chose leaders in cooperation with the Holy Spirit and then collectively appointed the new leaders and mediators in the different churches as they successively grew and matured in the Lord.

When a leader was identified and was mature enough and clearly met the moral and leadership qualifications, which was an absolute requirement in the early church (see chapter 13) they were then appointed into their respective position and roll. Nowhere in the Bible do the church members vote on who is supposed to be their leader or who should have that roll.

The collective leadership in and of itself is a safety factor that assures that the leader among leaders does not go off the deep end. A leader of leaders cannot make a decision that contradicts the other leaders. I, Johannes, am the ultimate leader for the Amritzer family, but I would not want to make a decision concerning the family or leading the family in a certain direction if Maria and I were not in agreement with each other. The church is not a company, business or sports club, but a great big spiritual family.

When it comes to choosing leaders in the different functions and areas of the church it is important to give way to those who have the gifting, talent and anointing for the task at hand. Not everyone is to lead worship since not everyone can sing. Some are good with numbers and can do bookkeeping and budgets easily while others are multi-gifted linguists who speak and write eight languages.

One of the leader's greatest tasks is to maximize other people and make sure that they use the gifts and talents that God has put inside of them. It is not mean or unfair for a worship leader to lovingly tell someone that they cannot sing and should try doing something else instead. It is quite the opposite. It should be freeing for someone who doesn't quite have clear self insight.

A leader who brings someone forward who has great gifting and anointing for the task is not favoring that person, as some people might think, but is recognizing and backing up what God has already put in them. To give way to someone who is gifted and anointed by God in different areas is to submit to authority and receive the gifts that God has blessed to the department. To stubbornly maintain fairness to all when the gifts and anointing of the other is apparent to everyone, is immature and a bad allocation and a waste of the resources and talents given directly from heaven.

Let Julia, Linnea, Nancy and Jenny sing. They can sing. They can sing and they are anointed by God to do it. Anna and Maria should dance. They have rhythm in their blood and are anointed by God for dance and choreography. Malin, Samuel and Rickard are excellent at layout and design; therefore they should do just that. Emil is great at drama and has incredible facial expressions. I don't mean that you cannot sing, dance or paint just for the fun of it even if you are not super gifted at it, but maybe not be on the stage doing it. Sing, dance, paint, sculpture if it makes you happy!

Every gift that has its proper place in the body of Christ, company or organization should be obvious. Equally important, not everyone should be doing everything. It is also important in the New Testament church life not to allow gifts that are without anointing and spiritual presence to lead. Prayer, fasting, concentration and right motives release the Holy Spirit's anointing over a gift in your life. We always say here at Mission SOS that concentration is anointing. Yes, it is actually true that concentration releases the presence of God. God's Spirit comes strongly when we are concentrated, dedicated and aware of what we are doing and totally focused on glorifying Him.

In Mission SOS we allow you to be as talented as you want, but if your life does not back up and confirm what you do and the leadership does not feel the presence of God and anointing over your gift, then we will not appoint you as a leader for that service.

Anointing is more important than gifting, knowledge and talents. Anointing and power without a holy, humble lifestyle and character to back it up is as dangerous as putting a gun in the hands of a five year old. The balance between talents or gifting, anointing or spiritual presence, character or maturity is very important and usually the anointing makes all the difference. If you are a potential leader and have leadership capabilities, then you most likely already know it because you just can't help but lead. Continue to be humble and bold, your time will come!

Chapter 3

THE PRICE OF LEADERSHIP

*"Whatever Saul sent him to do, David did it so suc-
cessfully that Saul gave him a high rank in the army.
This pleased all the people, and Saul's officers as well."*

1 Samuel 18:5

After the young David had slain the Philistine giant
Goliath and together with Israel conquered their enemies,
he became King Saul's chief commanding officer for a short
time. He had success and was appreciated. When the soldiers
came home from the war the Jewish women would come out
to meet them joyfully singing and dancing with tambourines
and lutes. They danced, they sang:

*"Saul has slain his thousands, and David his tens of
thousands."*

1 Samuel 18:7b

King Saul felt threatened by the young David's popularity and became angry, frightened and jealous. From that day onward he kept a jealous eye on David (1 Sam. 18:9). Saul tried to kill David several times and persecuted him for the rest of his life.

"When Saul saw how successful he was, he was afraid of him. But all Israel and Judah loved David, because he led them in their campaigns."
1 Samuel 18:15-16

David was forced to live with Saul's constant harassment, conspiracies, slander and gossip until Saul was ultimately slain in battle and David became the new King.

A true leader has an attractive force and ability to gather people to him. He is like a large magnet among small bits of metal, nuts and bolts. An immature leader can perceive a great leader as a threat instead of the gift he is. The great leader can struggle with the feeling of being a bull in a china shop. The leader feels hemmed in, suffocated and afraid of pulling out all the stops in the little context he is in since he most likely would blow up both house and church if he would start working at his full capacity and strength.

A great leader with no space to grow or expand for his capacity gets bored very quickly. There have been many leaders who have left the body of Christ simply because they were not given the space and task that matched their large personalities, but instead were seen as threats by pastors. A true spiritual leader must unfortunately learn to live with fear, jealousy and anger from those around him. Unfortunately, it is the price that has to be paid in order to be a pioneer and an influential leader. The price is often fear, jealousy and anger from the religious self appointed elite.

God help us to be generous and bighearted! Help us to be a creative greenhouse for great talents and leaders instead of being fearful and killers of spiritual gifts. God keep us from the religious mafia fighting over being the boss's favorite. In the 1930's and 40's Europe, Germans were afraid of the Jews. The Jews were a gift to Europe, smart, well-educated, gifted and wealthy artisans with strong personalities. The Germans murdered and gassed the Jews to death because they saw them as a threat against the Arian race, instead of a gift to it. What a horrible crime and mistake against the development and well-being of Europe. Maybe we would have had the USA's position and place of blessing and influence in the world today if we had let the Jews develop, blossom and live among us. I am convinced that we would have a much better Europe today if the Jews had been allowed to live and continue to bless us, and the world.

When denominations and the religious Saul leaders stir up people into a witch hunt of young leaders with power to break through, especially apostles, church planters, and prophets in Europe today, there are great consequences. If they look on the big personalities as a threat instead of a blessing, the future well-being and development of the Christian church is definitely threatened. Wake up! Stop smothering and executing the sharp and colorful youth pastors! Stop shooting down church planters and spiritual pioneers! If Christianity is to survive we need to have a generous Christian climate.

Someone needs to lead and pave the way where there is no way. Someone needs to be willing to get a few scratches and have their toes stepped on when we are fighting to make our way through a territory where no one has gone before. Someone needs to be prepared to kill a snake and scare away a panther or tiger. Some have died as spiritual explorers but in so doing made it easier for the rest of us who follow, to continue the trip and go longer and farther into unknown territory. Uncharted territories are to be conquered! Trips into uncharted and unreached areas are to be made. We need spiritual Christopher Columbus kinds of people in order to make it better for a people who are living in spiritual poverty. Someone needs to dare to sail into an uncertain horizon with his soul in his hands. We need pioneers and apostles more than ever.

A good pastor friend and colleague from Sweden said to me once, "If you could have just refrained from saying and speaking out certain things you would be a great spiritual leader in Sweden by now."

Your fruit and the level of your influence is what measures greatness, not necessarily how popular you are. I want to please God in the task He has given me to do. Others can determine what is great or not. The problem is not that I can't keep quiet about certain things, even if I actually should keep my mouth shut sometimes. The biggest problem is that too many people are just that: quiet. Unfortunately, too few are willing to pay the price and speak truths that need to be established, despite what the majority thinks and screams with threats. We need leaders that cannot be muzzled and bribed. We need men and women who are passionate about holding up the truth and willing to give their lives for it.

Some truths need to be clubbed through and established even through hard attacks. Truths like the reality of demons and the need for deliverance. So many are longing for the gospel but don't want to be part of a powerless and boring church. God wants to heal everyone. Jesus still baptizes in the Holy Spirit and fire. We cannot compromise these truths!

Homosexuality, sodomy, incest and pornography are a perversion and are sin. Abortion is the murder of innocent unborn children. Alcohol and drugs are a curse for a nation and people that we need to fight for with every means possible! Truths like the ones I just mentioned don't change just because society changes and becomes more liberal through the years.

Spiritual maturity is not that as the years go by you drift further away from the Word of God, but instead, spiritual maturity is actively defending and guarding the truths of the Bible. Truths are not invalidated just because we keep quiet. They get lost and forgotten about in the frayed and deteriorated minds of people today. We need to be shouting from the housetops absolutes like reaping and sowing, sin and righteousness again! Timid and cowardly leaders are a shame to the Christian church, the business community and politics!

"Even when their drinks are gone, they continue their prostitution; their rulers dearly love shameful ways."

Hosea 4:18

It is worth it to pay a higher price for strong leadership. The price can never be too high for the salvation of our land and people! Who is willing to pay a higher price for stronger and bolder leadership? Churches need to be larger and have more influence on society. Christian businessmen need to be successful and earn lots of money. How else are we to successfully win the people for Jesus and finish the task of the Great Commission?

Chapter 4

COVENANT FRIENDSHIPS

However contradictory it may seem, Prince Jonathan, King Saul's son, and David were best friends, covenant friends.

"And Jonathan made a covenant with David because he loved him as himself."

1 Samuel 18:3

David and Jonathan really loved each other as real blood brothers do and entered into covenant with each other. Jonathan said:

"May the Lord call David's enemies to account."

1 Samuel 20:16b

David's enemies were Jonathans enemies and vice versa. For a long period of time David lived in exile. He was pursued by King Saul and his soldiers and for survival he was hiding out in the desert and the wild. At one point when David was close to giving up, he felt discouraged, sad and dejected he met Jonathan in a secret meeting place out in the desert. It says:

> *"And Saul's son Jonathan went to David at Horesh*
> *in the Desert of Ziph and helped him find strength in*
> *God."*

1 Samuel 23:16

We need friends who can strengthen us in the Lord when needed. A leader needs what I usually call covenant friendships, other leaders who live the same lifestyle, who know and understand each other. People with the same spiritual DNA-code enjoy each other's company. A common, radical Christian lifestyle and a common goal unites and creates the feeling of solidarity.

Every leader needs this type of generous and warm friendship with others who are like-minded. We do not need friends that just cry, sigh and speak unbelief to us when the going gets tough. Let's not fall into the trap of singing old and nostalgic battle songs from times gone by and only talk of the good ole' days when we meet. We all need to watch out that we don't end up there as the years go by, we need to constantly keep ourselves current, never ceasing to be a pioneer.

We most certainly need covenant friendships with people who can wipe away our tears, but also can stand with us and shout to the Lord in prayer. I will never forget a friend who cried together with me first then he threw himself on me and prayed and shouted to God that my depression would leave and thank God it did! Thank God for such friends, real fellow-soldiers. Friends who know how to comfort, but also really give practical help in a time of need. Fellow pastor friends, business leaders, yes, real partners who take up an offering when you need money to pay for your pending bills. Friends who clean and wash your car and iron your shirts when you and your wife have worked around the clock and still haven't caught up with your own lives. Friends you can call at 3 o'clock in the morning and say, "Help me!" They are standing ten minutes later outside your door and don't think that losing one night of sleep is such a big deal. Friendship is so much more valuable.

When Jonathan was killed on mount Gilboa in the battle against the Philistines, David sang a song of mourning, at the end of the song he sings:

> *"I grieve for you, Jonathan my brother; you were*
> *very dear to me. Your love for me was wonderful,*
> *more wonderful than that of women."*
> **2 Samuel 1:26**

No pastor in Sweden has ever meant as much to me personally than Pastor Sven Bengtsson. Sven's wife Vicky is also a great friend to my wife Maria. We have prayed, fasted and cried together. We speak faith, stand in faith and encourage each other. We spur on, encourage and sharpen each other all the time.

"As iron sharpens iron, so one man sharpens another."

Proverbs 27:17

"A man of many companions may come to ruin, but there is a friend who sticks closer than a brother."

Proverbs 18:24

Sven has taught me more than anyone else. Sven has taught me to keep the Sabbath day holy, which is actually the third of the Ten Commandments. I need to put this into practice for Maria, the children and my own sake. The Bengtsson family is our foremost example on child-raising and also on how to rest and relax in God. Sven and Vicky's faith in God and His promises have rubbed off on us and have made a great impression in our hearts. They have been wonderful and secure leaders for the Amritzer family, the leadership team, and the congregation at Harvest Center, where Mission SOS made up the mission's department for several years.

The years when I was Mission's Director and Assistant Pastor together with Sven at Harvest Center was the best time of my life. He and Vicky are great gifts to the Amritzer family. Without them Mission SOS would never have been able to do what we are doing now in our work to the unreached people groups. Sven is a true covenant friend.

God has really blessed me and graciously given me real covenant friends like Peter Almqvist, Per Gisselsson, Andreas Gustafsson, Per-Olof Eurell, John-Ted Berge, Walter Zuniga,

Asokan PK, Ari Mathiesen, among others. Thanks for being part of my life! Without you life would be so much poorer and more difficult. You were given to me as gifts directly from God and therefore I can live and continue to preach the gospel with full strength. With friends like you life is so much more fun and fulfilling. You are all my covenant friends and I truly love you all from the depths of my heart!

Chapter 5

OFFENSE IS THE BEST DEFENSE

When David had become a great and notorious warrior king he made the mistake of starting to live on past merits and yesterday's victories. David was successful and had prosperity in everything he did. He suppressed all of his enemies around Israel. David created national security, prosperity and safe boarders for his people and country. David became greater than any king before or after his reign.

> *"The Lord gave David victory wherever he went."*
> **2 Samuel 8:6b**

But then…

> *"In the spring, at the time when kings go off to war, David sent Joab out with the king's men and the*

*whole Israelite army. They destroyed the Ammonites
and besieged Rabbah. But David remained in
Jerusalem."*

2 Samuel 11:1

It says, at the time when kings go off to war. Every year, at a specific time, all the kings would go off to war. Instead, King David sent his Commander-in-chief Joab out with all of his men, but he himself stayed home in Jerusalem. What happened here? The warrior king stopped fighting. David was tired, slacking off and starting to lose touch, but he still was holding up an image that everything was as usual. He never should have stayed at home. It was the beginning of the end of a fantastic era of success and victory for King David. We further read:

*"One evening David got up from his bed and
walked around on the roof of the palace. From the
roof he saw a woman bathing. The woman was very
beautiful…"*

2 Samuel 11:2

Well, that's how it goes when you start sleeping all day and are awake at night, like a teenager who has had summer vacation for too long without a summer job. It was clear that the king was no longer getting up early to work out at the gym or out running in the early mornings. He slept late into the afternoon and then went around in sweat pants and a T-shirt and slippers out on the terrace. David had taken off his armor and was showing his scars and the tattoos on his upper arms, telling war-stories for the young servants in his household, within the safe, thick and secure walls of Jerusalem. He was far away from the battlefield and the besiegement of Rabbah, while his war heroes were shedding their blood for Israel far away from their leader and mentor. Being a deserter, a spirit of laziness had come over the middle-aged former warrior, King David.

He spots a woman from the terrace of his palace. She was beautiful in the evening sun as the sparkling water poured over her body. David could not take his eyes off of her but was gripped with an overwhelming surge of lust and was left standing there staring with his mouth hung open. He consumed her with his eyes and since he no longer was in a state of alertness and discipline he fell into temptation. He asked one of the servants to find out who the young woman was and discovered that she was the wife of Uriah, one of his most faithful soldiers. Despite the fact that he knew she was Uriah's wife, he did not hesitate to have sex with her.

Bathsheba got pregnant. When the king received the news that Bathsheba was with child, he sent for Uriah to quickly come home from battle. David hoped to get him so drunk that he would go home and sleep with his wife. In a last attempt to save his own skin he tried to get Uriah to spend at least one night with his wife. Despite all of the King's plans, this warrior still had so much self-control that he refused to sleep anywhere else than among the servants, at the gate of the king. Uriah was only on a short visit to Jerusalem, in fact, it was only for two nights. He wanted to remain loyal to his troops. His heart was on the battlefield. No matter how tempting the idea of being in his wife's arms might be, he chose not to go home; a true warrior.

Uriah was sent back into battle at the besiegement of the city of Rabbah with his own death warrant, in the form of a letter to Joab, his Commander-in-chief. In the letter David ordered Joab to send Uriah into the frontlines where the fighting was fiercest, and then draw back without him to let him be struck down by the enemy.

As soon as David got word that Uriah was dead, murdered, he sent for Bathsheba. She became his wife and gave birth to a son. Bathsheba was not David's wife. Bathsheba is not your wife either, she belongs to someone else! You the reader may need to stop and ask yourself this question; "Is there a Bathsheba in my life?"

In this specific case it wasn't Bathsheba that was the problem, but David's laziness and backslidden state. David stopped fighting. He was in the wrong place at the wrong time. On the frontlines of the battlefield, Bathsheba bathing naked is not a film that is being shown. It is only being shown in an outdoor theater on the terrace roof of a backslider in Jerusalem. These performances, shows and perversities follow and succeed each other in the camp of a lazy pacifist.

A warrior fights. A warrior who has stopped fighting is not a warrior at all. A soldier is trained to use his weapons and to go out into battle. A boxer boxes, otherwise we call him a former boxer. A leader leads. Are you possibly a former leader? Are you a former warrior? A leader only continues to be a good leader and fighter when he is out into battle with regularity. If he is at home he is resting and recuperating for new conquests for the Kingdom of God. The apostle Paul says to his spiritual son Timothy:

> *"Endure hardship with us like a good soldier of*
> *Christ Jesus."*
> **2 Timothy 2:3**

It is dangerous to be a living legend. To have hero status after your death must be better than getting medals for bravery and going into retirement as a veteran soldier and then continuing to live many more years after that. The kingdom of God has no retirees or war-veterans. We are instead like airplanes that hold their highest speed just before take-off and we lift and leave this earth for our heavenly home. There are many battles to be won. There are many people groups that still have not heard the good news of Jesus Christ. The Great Commission is still in effect. Join the army again! Start working out again! We need you on the battlefield!

At the end of your life as a leader you should be able to say with the apostle Paul:

> *"I have fought the good fight, I have finished the*
> *race, I have kept the faith."*
> **2 Timothy 4:7**

In Mission SOS we clearly notice how quickly a leader becomes slack and dulled when it has been a long time since he was out in the field on a festival. When a leader is not taking part in the different mission's trips, evangelization or the practical follow-up of new converts he starts getting critical and whiney. Every Christian leader needs to have fellowship with unbelievers and constantly live in an outgoing and soul-winning life so as to not lose his edge and focus. Offense is always the best defense. Never stop fighting! Conquer! Be on the offense!

Be cautious of David!

David fell because of laziness, slackness and a lack of discipline. Be cautious of a backslidden leader who entices and manipulates with his gifts and talents. A slacking David gift on the slide can most certainly be the fall of many people with its confidence, experience and fatherly charm. It doesn't always have to be about sexual sin but can also involve the opportunity that one is deceived and lets down his integrity and principles. No one is so strong that he is untouchable or invulnerable to the attacks of the devil. The devil will sneak up from behind like the Asian mafia and entangle you when you least expect it.

Keep a good distance if you sense unclean vibes from another leader of the opposite sex. Sometimes the world's Bathshebas are not totally innocent either, so you will need to be alert if you are walking in David's shoes as well. Most certainly a little Bathsheba will try to bathe outside your window or in your backyard if you do not have enough character to back away. This is living dangerously. It doesn't matter if the guy looks as innocent as Peter Pan or the girl as Tinker Bell, watch out! Working together in a team is hard because you become close friends and share so much with someone who is not your husband or wife. A strong woman leader must be on the alert as much as a man. Leadership in itself is attractive; and as mentioned previously a leader will attract people to them.

At Mission SOS we currently have approximately 170 young leaders in the ages between 20 and 35 all over the world. We clearly teach and emphasize these principles in a practical way. We work in teams both at home and abroad on the mission field and are always saying: Be careful for David! Watch out for Bathsheba! In that order!

> *"For the lips of an adulteress drip honey, and her speech is smoother than oil; but in the end she is bitter as gall, sharp as a double-edged sword. Her feet go to death; her steps lead straight to the grave."*
>
> **Proverbs 5:3-5**

Don't forget that offense is always the best defense even when it comes to lust! The few times I have been sexually tempted, I bow my knees and pray in tongues and speak to the spirit of lust, and it usually works. If not, I call my wife on my cell phone and we pray together, that is a sure thing! Unclean spirits do not like to be put in the light. The last mentioned I have only needed to do a couple of times, during my 14 years of marriage.

That I actually feel quite strong in this area must be because I have such a beautiful wife, so just the thought of her usually scares the temptation and devil away. You cannot be careful enough in this area nor have too high boundaries. Be cautious for David! Watch out for Bathsheba!

Chapter 6

CHOOSE IN HOUSE LEADERS

King David had his group of mighty men to surround him, strong leaders that stood with him during the tough times, in defeat but also through the victories. They were the mighty men of David. They were mighty because of David, and he became the king of Israel because of them. Each of their individual successes and assignments were closely and intimately tied to one other.

> *"These were the chiefs of David's mighty men-they, together with all Israel, gave his kingship strong support to extend it over the whole land, as the Lord had promised"*
>
> **1 Chronicles 11:10**

Once when David's hometown of Bethlehem was occupied by the Philistine garrison, David said longingly:

"Oh, that someone would get me a drink of water
from the well near the gate of Bethlehem!"

1 Chronicles 11:17

Three of the thirty chiefs broke through the Philistine lines, drew water from the well near the gate of Bethlehem and carried it back to David. But David refused to drink it; instead he poured it out as an offering before the Lord. What incredible leaders! What mighty men! David wanted to drink water from the well in his hometown and his closest chiefs risked their lives, put everything on the line to go and retrieve a little water for David to drink.

They loved David. Men came from Benjamin's and Judah's tribe to join David while he was still in exile and being pursued. David wondered if they had come with peaceful intentions when he met them outside his fort. One of the mighty men put it so well when he answered David's inquiry:

"Then the Spirit came upon Amasai, chief of the
Thirty, and he said: We are yours, O David! We are
with you, O son of Jesse! Success, success to you,
and success to those who help you, for your God will
help you."

1 Chronicles 12:18

According to the words of Jesus in the Great Commission, we are all called to make disciples, right? A great leader will soon build his leadership team and it is important they think correctly. It is in the nature of a leader to multiply what is within himself; many more leaders will be born successively if they are healthy, life-giving churches, organizations and companies. Maria and I have two children. Many people say that they are very much like their mother and for that I am very grateful to God, but some things they have gotten from their dad too, and it is quite obvious…

> *"I praise you because I am fearfully and wonderfully made…"*
> **Psalm 139:14a**

If the children were not anything like us, that would be very strange. Children usually turn out like their parents.

> *"Sons are a heritage from the Lord, children a reward from him."*
> **Psalm 127:3**

When Israel's forefather Abram went into battle against the men of Kedorlaomer in order to rescue his nephew Lot, he chose his most prominent men:

> *"…he called out the 318 trained men born in his household…"*
> **Genesis 14:14**

Out of all of Abram's many servants, he chose his most faithful and trusted ones, those born in his own household, when he was going out into battle. Likewise, when you are going to go into spiritual battle you really need to have your family around you.

Apostolic leadership is something I really love, proclaim and believe in. It can be summed up in one word; fatherhood. It is about taking responsibility, ownership and loyalty. An apostolic leader gradually learns to give other leaders born in the house or through his ministry the leading positions and trusted assignments. For me this lesson came at a high price that I have had to learn a few times over in the past years.

It doesn't matter how good of friends we are, or what opinions we have, when I am going to choose a leader it is one that is born in this house. Who are they? Our own disciples in the faith, but also our Bible school graduates. I willingly work together with wonderful pastors, leaders and business men throughout the whole world on common projects and ventures like festivals, seminars, conferences, book projects, the spreading of Bibles and other literature, and social benefits for society. However, the leaders I choose in Mission SOS are only the ones that are born within the house or those that have chosen to be adopted by us after a year of Bible school at Mission SOS or have stood with us over a long period of time and have shown their loyalty and commitment to the ministry. The apostle Paul says this about his spiritual son Timothy:

> "I have no one else like him, who takes a genuine
> interest in your welfare. For everyone looks out for

his own interests, not those of Jesus Christ. But you
know that Timothy has proved himself because as a
son with his father he has served with me in the work
of the gospel."

Philippians 2:20-22

The apostle Paul also says about Philemon and Apphia's escaped slave Onesimus, whom he led to Jesus during his house arrest in Rome:

"I appeal to you for my son Onesimus, who became
my son while I was in chains."

Philemon 1:10

When the apostle Paul is to send Onesimus from Rome to Asia to his former owner Philemon, he says this:

"I am sending him who is my very heart back to
you."

Philemon 1:12

The apostle Paul gave birth to spiritual children in Christ and became attached to them, they were like his very own children and he took responsibility for them. Paul then says in the letter to Philemon about Onesimus:

"So if you consider me a partner, welcome him as
you would welcome me."

Philemon 1:17

Apostolic leadership is fantastic because it gets rid of so called employed pastors that can be kicked out or fired when the church doesn't like what they do. In a family you cannot fire or kick out your mother or father. Your children will always be your children no matter what. An apostolic leader does not change families when the going gets tough or if a better opportunity arises. He has given birth to others so he needs to take care of the ones he loves. If the parent does his job right the child knows who his real parents are.

I have never been the least bit afraid that those with strong ministry gifts visiting Mission SOS or one of our bases or churches around the world could steal our children. Our children know where they belong and what they are to prioritize. Only the leaders and pastors who are hired are the ones who are insecure. At our place we welcome strong ministry gifts to preach, dance and explode. We keep that promise!

All revivals and spiritual movements have their own leaders. The followers are in a way, baptized into them. It is completely natural and right. This is what it says about the people of Israel:

> "They were all baptized into Moses in the cloud and in the sea. They all ate the same spiritual food and drank the same spiritual drink; for they drank from the spiritual rock that accompanied them, and that rock was Christ."
>
> **1 Corinthians 10:2-4**

Baptized into Moses? Yeah, that's just what it says. An old Swedish Pentecostal woman was baptized into the Pentecostal revival that came through Lewi Pethrus. And the Word of Life follower, who was baptized into the wild pioneer spirit from the 1980's in Sweden, will always stand together with Ulf Ekman, who is the founder and father of this movement, and it should be that way.

We are bearing children! We have gone through the same baptism, we eat the same spiritual food and drink the same spiritual drink. We are all Indians but some belong to the Sioux tribe and others to the Apache tribe. Jesus, however, is everyone's chief. We can definitely join together to do things, when we need to fight common enemies!

God has given us many mighty men in Mission SOS and oh how we love them - Stephanie and Daniel Elvelyck, Anna and Jonathan Kvist, Samuel and Julia Willkander, Maria Jonson and many, many others. They are all born in this house or have let themselves be adopted by us, because they love Mission SOS.

Chapter 7

LEADERS ARE BORN ON THE BATTLEFIELD

King David's mighty men were not guys with fancy titles who sat around reading the debate pages in the Jerusalem Post and pushing papers around a dusty office. David's mighty men were called mighty because they had accomplished heroic feats and efforts in battle. All of them earned their title and hero status on the battlefield. The Bible says the following about David's mighty men:

"...they were armed with bows and were able to shoot arrows or to sling stones right-handed or left-handed."

1 Chronicles 12:2

"Some Gadites defected to David at his stronghold in the desert. They were brave warriors, ready for battle and able to handle the shield and spear.

Their faces were the faces of lions, and they were as
swift as gazelles in the mountains."

1 Chronicles 12:8

A fair description and teaching of David's mighty men could easily fill a whole book alone. I am just going to mention a few things here to help you understand how David became such a great and influential leader. David was great himself, but he also dared to surround himself with leaders who were actually better and stronger than himself in different areas. They had specific expertise that far exceeded his. For example:

Josheb-Basshebeth, one of David's mighty men, was extremely skilled in using his sword and spear and most likely was more skillful than David in this specific area.

"He raised his spear against eight hundred men,
whom he killed in one encounter."

2 Samuel 23:8b

Eleazar had incredible stamina and persistence that far outweighed everyone else's. He was a master with the sword; he fought, slashed and struck the enemy:

"...but he stood his ground and struck down the
Philistines till his hand grew tired and froze to the
sword."

2 Samuel 23:10

Can you hear the guys, hours after the battle, laughing and patting Eleazar on the back that evening by the campfire as they were trying to remove the sword that was frozen to his hand? Eleazar was a mighty man that never gave up, never gave in. The laughing probably continued among them as they tried to get the muscles in his stiff, cramped hand and arms to relax and start to function normally.

Massaging, oils, pats on the back and a few raw but encouraging gibes and laughter from the other mighty men was something that united them forever. Friends that are bound together through warfare, tough conditions and even some bloodshed together, stay together. They have seen each other's best and worst sides. They have been completely transparent to one another and have spent time together. They are blood brothers, warrior brothers and know that they are fighting in David's and the Lord of Hosts, God Almighty's army!

The mighty man Shammah defended a field of lentils (2 Samuel 23:11-12). He stood completely alone in the middle of the field and fought off the Philistines and won a victory.

"...and the Lord brought about a great victory."
2 Samuel 23:12b

Shammah knew who gave the victory. He gave God the glory for it! Abishai raised his spear and slew over three hundred men and his name was well respected (2 Samuel 23:18). Benaiah was another brave man in David's elite troop who did many great deeds.

*"He also went down into a pit on a snowy day and
killed a lion."*

2 Samuel 23:20b

Wow, what a gang! It's not strange that David became the man he did and went down as Israel's greatest king through history. He was surrounded and backed up by heroes.

A leader must be someone who does more than just administrate the forefather's inheritance and devote himself to renew and polish the old instead of giving birth to something new. We need leaders who can fight in prayer and breakthrough in the assignments of Jesus' commission to make disciples. A leader in the kingdom of God prays with people to salvation and gives birth, forms and brings up disciples to Jesus. A spiritual leader helps people to receive baptism in the Holy Spirit's power and fire.

Our leaders in Mission SOS pray for the sick and cast out demons with great success. They are all born on our Jesus festivals among Muslims, Hindus and Buddhists. They are leaders who are born on the battlefield, festivals and prayer school in Märsta or on an outreach in Northern Stockholm. They preach the gospel on the subway or during a culture-exchange party. Missionaries at our bases are all warriors who serve a great and living God!

Lead By What They Have Performed

David's leaders became leaders based on their performance in battle, rather than the right connections, family or knowing how to act politically correct. When David was to attack and occupy the Jebusites city, he said:

> *"Whoever leads the attack on the Jebusites will become commander-in-chief."*
> **1 Chronicles 11:6**

Joab, the son of Zeruiah, came up first and so became commander-in-chief of David's army. Joab was very successful in battle. He took up David's challenge and was the first one to occupy Jebus, the future city of Jerusalem. He was then promoted. David thought as any leader should think, "Who can get the job done?" The one who gives the most, gets the most. The one who stakes the most gets the reward and gets the trustworthy positions.

With great passion and a willingness to fight, you can go farther than having lots of talent and knowledge. David did not show partiality towards anyone. Ancestors and merit lists from the past did not make any difference in David's troops. What you actually could do out on the field was what determined your roll, position and rank.

Martina Almqvist and **Marielle Gisselsson** are two heroines in Mission SOS. Both were born out of prayer, spiritual warfare and on the wild pioneer mission adventures. They were single when they came to us and today they are both married and mothers of several children. Martina and Marielle have prayed together with Maria and me more than anyone else in the Mission SOS team because they were the first two full time co-workers. We usually met early in the morning at our office in Jönköping and prayed for two hours before we started working. We also met together in the evenings at our apartment and prayed, sang worship songs and prayed again. We have bent over maps, photographs of ethnic groups and peoples crying and shouting out to God, breaking only to take a glass of water. Those years in Jönköping were where and how Mission SOS was born.

Martina and Marielle traveled around Sweden and presented SOS. They led in prayer for the unreached people groups; sometimes without receiving a travel allowance or paid expenses from the churches they visited. The Amritzer family, Martina Roobert, Marielle Engström and the Widell family from Ryd were Mission SOS those first few years. Together we made many spiritual discovery trips. There were long fasts and prayer nights together and we baptized many former Animists and tribal people in different rivers together.

My wife Maria, Martina and Marielle cast out many demons. They were always in the demon clinic, the little tent behind the platform, where we usually carried the demon possessed for deliverance and prayer. When I preached the evil spirits almost always started screaming and going berserk with their poor victims. Strong men helped to carry them out of the public's eye. There the SOS girls took over and worked on them. Their authority was like whipping and slashing after all the days of fasting and hours spent together with God in prayer. The demons fled at the name of Jesus and many changes in regiments of power took place. The girls can tell their stories if you dare to listen. Then, of course, they have shopped together, oh boy, have they done some shopping in all the market places of Manila, New Delhi, and Karachi, to name a few! Today, they are all mature women of God and pillars in our organization, our own heroines and SOS mothers!

Peter Almqvist is our own MacGyver. He is a living, multi-tool handyman. He knows everything from computers, sound and lighting equipment, cars and even exchange rates. He is a tough general at our festivals and sleeps the least of everyone during warfare. He can speak English better than Swedish, speaks Urdu and understands Hindi. Peter never ceases to surprise and amaze me. When he and I have slept in our sleeping bags on the platform of the indoor arenas, or outdoors on a terrace in Ethiopia, I have really come to respect him. He is always up early in the morning praying and reading his Bible. He starts working before all of us. He is a workhorse, a warrior and a hero. I feel comfortable with Peter in times of war or on any battlefront.

The same thing goes for **Per Gisselsson** and **Walter Zuniga**, two of Mission SOS' field directors. They were not born in Christian conferences, rather out on the battlefield in the dust and dirt of missions work.

In 2000, Per and I spent a night on the streets of Gävle, there I discovered what he was made of. After Per had preached the Gospel to a girl in the drug quarter, we were offered the worst cup of coffee I have ever tasted in my life! I knew then that we were blood brothers. Then in the early morning hours, when Per led another drunken, beaten girl to salvation outside of the disco tech, I knew...

"Per, would you like to work with me? Would you like to share your life as an evangelist with me?"

The questions popped out of me quickly and he responded immediately to my offer. Love at first sight? No, but after seeing him take care of drunkards in their vomit and profuse nosebleeds and coffee that had been in the pot for three days, a life-long, loving friendship was a fact. Today, Per leads our mission base in Southeast Asia together with his wife Marielle, in the city of Khon Kaen in Thailand. Together with his bold team he preaches the Gospel in Vietnam, Laos and Cambodia.

During a mission trip to Ecuador, Walter led a taxi chauffeur to salvation in the capital city of Quito. Later, when we had a flat tire, Walter continued to preach. You can't stop an anointed Latino-evangelist who has gotten a foot in the door. He latches on like a pit-bull terrier. Walter led the guy to baptism in the Holy Spirit and speaking in tongues all the while the taxi chauffeur was changing the tires on his car. When we finally arrived at the church where I was to preach Walter was to pay, and our taxi chauffer was so intoxicated by the Holy Spirit that he could not stop speaking in tongues. It was then I knew that Walter was a true hero and a little brother to me! Walter and his wife Linda lead our mission base in the Balkan Peninsula and they are fantastic team builders and church planters.

Emma Gustafsson was born as an SOS hero on the roof of a jeep in the Philippine jungle in 2001. When it happened, I saw it, and I knew it at once. Suddenly, her eyes were filled with tears and she knew that together with us, she was to give her life for the unreached peoples. She held on tightly and desperately to the roof, her hair was blown to and fro in the wind and she laughed and cried and enjoyed life.

February 2001, in a chilly cold Turkish part of Bulgaria, **Andreas Gustafsson**, Emma's husband, and our dear Finance Manager, was born into Mission SOS with a Turkish cup of coffee in his hand. Andreas loves to pray for the Middle East; Muslim men with mustaches, and the Persian and Turkish food culture. Andreas knows the Prophet Muhammad's life history almost as well as the Gospels of Jesus and knows a lot of unimportant stuff about Kalifer (Islamic political leaders), strange Muslim factions and terrorist organizations. Andreas dream about Kaddafi's and Hassan Nassralah's salvations and will not give up until the early church is restored even geographically.

Maria Evermin is an SOS girl in a class by herself. Despite the fact that she only has shoe size 4, she stands solid with both feet on the ground. It doesn't matter what task we give her, she does it with excellence and follows it through with a military authority, or shall we say a former KGB's accuracy. She is fantastic and works constantly, almost too much! Whether it is copying cassettes or CD-teachings, boring administrative office jobs, making and setting up creative drama and street theater dramas, she is always happy, laughing and full of life. If allowed by the love of her life, her husband Ante, Maria would sleep in a sleeping bag under the festival stage.

In March 2004, during a festival in South Kenya, I knew without a doubt that **Julia Willkander** qualified and merited to be Music Director in Mission SOS. How? I was standing parallel to the platform, just outside the stairs, waiting to come up and preach. Julia sang, danced and led the Kenyan audience of 15,000 people in wild worship. She laughed and shouted and got the audience going even between the songs with all of her charming stage presence. What a powerful presence of God she released as she sang.

Right in the middle of a song Julia waves to the rest of the singers and band to continue. With a big smile on her face she says in the microphone, "Take the chorus one more time!" She then raced down the stairs, pushed me out of the way and stood behind the platform and vomited. There she was, the artist and singer, Julia, trying not to throw up on her shoes, blouse and dress! Yeah, I was impressed. I knew that many in the team had the stomach flu, but I didn't notice a trace of it in Julia until she ran down the stairs from the platform. What self-control! The story doesn't end there. Julia dried off her mouth, asked those of us standing by if she had anything left on her face. When we shook our heads at her she ran up the stairs and once again took the microphone like nothing had happened. She continued to sing, dance and lead worship with all her might and perfect stage presence. That was when I knew, in that moment, that Julia was our future Director of Music in Mission SOS! That is the type of fighters that we want to work and associate ourselves with!

Marcus Johnsen is without a doubt one of my best street evangelists. When Marcus took over our Mission SOS Bible school Christmas party in 2003 and started preaching, praying and prophesying over us teachers, I knew and all of my other leaders knew that he was a guy we could count on. Marcus, I love you, you are a fantastic missionary and evangelist!

Quite recently, I saw a brand new hero here at Mission SOS, **Samuel Strandberg**, born as a hero on the battlefield. Despite his young age, he leads our work at our mission base in Ethiopia with excellence. Samuel is a true hero who loves the Somali desert.

Chapter 8

RELEASE AND LIBERATE LEADERS

All great leaders are generous. They have an attitude and a spirit over them that says, "You may work with me and my team if you want to, it's your choice and I bless you whatever you choose!" David did not take anything for granted. He went through too much persecution to do that. When David's son Absalom had conspired and devised plans to overthrow his reign, David left Jerusalem. Despite the fact that David was surrounded by all of his mighty men it did not hinder the man Shimei from loudly cursing the king:

> *"So David and his men continued along the road*
> *while Shimei was going along the hillside opposite*
> *him, cursing as he went and throwing stones at him*
> *and showering him with dirt."*
>
> **2 Samuel 16:13**

Abishai, one of the mighty men asked for the king's permission to chop off Shimei's head and said:

"Why should this dead dog curse my lord the king?"
2 Samuel 16:9

David would not allow it. He would rather have stones and insults thrown at him than to take justice into his own hands, use his power and waste his energy on the wrong thing.

Sometimes a leader is simply too big to remain in his context. He grows out of his clothes, hits the roof, so to speak and must move on. New families are then born and healthy branches are formed. Seeds from our tree can blow farther away and take root in a totally different place. It is so wonderful!

When someone wants to go on the only thing to do is to tip your hat, bless them and write nice letters of recommendation! To release and liberate leaders is the secret to great success for churches, organizations and companies. If the ones who leave are successful, they will be great and strong covenant partners in the future. Sister and daughter organizations are fantastic when facing battles on a national and international level. If they are not successful, then they have hopefully learned both humility and respect and will certainly come back to you if you blessed and loved them when they chose to leave. You of course, are waiting with open arms when they choose to come back. Don't say, "I told you." Know it all's, stingy and narrow minded leaders never become great.

In Exodus we read how one should treat the Hebrew slaves, who were more like servants. When a Hebrew slave had served his master for six years, on the seventh year he would be set free without needing to pay a fee. It says:

> *"But if the servant declares, "I love my master and*
> *my wife and children and do not want to go free,*
> *then his master must take him before the judges. He*
> *shall take him to the door or the doorpost and pierce*
> *his ear with an awl. Then he will be his servant for*
> *life."*

Exodus 21:5-6

You know, we always release and liberate leaders, but maybe they love us and the children and everything else we have done and experienced together so much that they choose to stay for life. They usually say with all their heart, "I want to stay with you!" Then we pierce their ear so to speak, and stand and serve together for a whole lifetime. I have many leaders who are bond servants to me, but I am also a bond servant to a special leader.

If someone says, "Shouldn't my loyalty be only to Jesus and not to anyone else?" Yes, of course, first to God, then your immediate family, but then you should give yourself to your setting or context in which you are involved. Don't be volatile and rootless, but decide, sooner rather than later, with whom you are going to stand.

"When you make a vow to God, do not delay in fulfilling it. He has no pleasure in fools; fulfill your vow."

Ecclesiastes 5:4

Maybe it is time to look up your former spiritual mother or father and say, "I love you, pierce my ear!"

Daniel Elvelyck, who today is Director of Mission SOS Sweden was saved and baptized as a 15 year old boy in one of my meetings in southern Sweden. Daniel made his trip away from us at Mission SOS for a short while, but then he came to us and said, "Pierce my ear! Mission SOS is my family forever!" He started as a street evangelist shortly after that and led our outreach and evangelization at SOS Mission Bible College for one and a half years, then started teaching at the school as one of the main teachers. What a gift of teaching, Daniel is the best we have! Daniel is so organized, a great administrator and has great leader potential. What a preacher! I want to listen to you Daniel! It feels so good to have you here at home with us.

Many of our most faithful co-workers have first made their trip through different churches or Christian organizations, and then, after awhile, they come back. Often that trip can take a year or two. It is good because it gives them perspective and hopefully births an even deeper love and respect for the family.

A leader's attitude must be one of blessing when someone wants to leave an organization or church. Sometimes it can be hard to disregard your own thoughts and plans for a spiritual son or daughter, but it is important to release people so that they can make their own trip with God. A true spiritual parent says, "No problem, we are here when you come back, if you come back." We are generous. We bless and are willing to share! No leader or spiritual parents own their children. The children are free and parents naturally want what is best for their children!

Chapter 9

GOOD ORGANIZATION AND COMMUNICATION

King David was not afraid of good organization. David organized the building of the temple long before Solomon started to build it. King Solomon, David's son and successor, built the temple after his father's death. David planned, organized and gathered building material, which was stored for his son's future construction of the temple. David even organized the temple services with its different departments. He decided who would serve during specific months and then succeed one another. The Levites, i.e. priests, temple singers, musicians and door keepers all had department chiefs and knew exactly what their title and task was and what time schedules they were to have.

David's warriors, or should we say army, naturally was also well organized. David took a census and registered the people of Israel by their size and with the name of the chief leader over their families. The army was organized with commanders and subordinates and department heads for the different regiments who served alternately during the year.

David had chief officers over all of his possessions and the treasures of the court. David organized his farms, vineyards, olive plantations and oil storage with different department heads and workers. David employed his uncle Jonathan and Ahithophel as his personal advisors and Joab was the commander of the royal army.

David went a little too far in his perfectionism and actually brought a curse and pestilence over the land of Israel at one point, because God did not like his motive behind the census of the people. David wanted to show the world how great his kingdom had become and this bragging stole glory from God. David had received everything from God – his leadership capabilities, administrative gifts and the people who served him. Everything he had was because of God's grace towards him.

Despite this, God is not against our organization, quite the contrary; he allows his blessing and favor to rest upon organization. The Bible tells about Moses building the tabernacle according to all the instructions and commands given to him by God. The following then happened:

> *"Then the cloud covered the Tent of Meeting, and the glory of the Lord filled the tabernacle."*
>
> **Exodus 40:34**

When King Solomon finished the building of the temple and had just finished his prayer at the inauguration ceremony the following happened:

> *"When Solomon finished praying, fire came down from heaven and consumed the burnt offering and the sacrifices, and the glory of the Lord filled the temple."*
>
> **2 Chronicles 7:1**

God loves peace and harmony, not cold, technical order. There doesn't have to be a conflict between good organization and a warm, loving style of leadership. I am convinced that these two elements can be joined together beautifully. When the prophet Joel described the end times' great army of the Lord and its organization he said:

> *"They charge like warriors; they scale walls like soldiers. They all march in line, not swerving from their course. They do not jostle each other; each marches straight ahead. They plunge through defenses without breaking ranks."*
>
> **Joel 2:7-8**

Everyone of them knew his place and path. A well organized army is an impressive sight. Strangely, it is just after this description the great prophecy comes describing the outpouring of the Spirit in the last days, with prophecies, dreams and visions at the end of Chapter 2 in the book of

Joel. First order and discipline, then there is the right conditions and channels for God's Spirit to work and flow. It is quite an exciting connection, I think.

A leadership that is afraid of good organization, order and discipline will never be able to be more than a small group activity; small and without any strong influence. Leadership that wants to accomplish much will need to be effective, multiplying and focused on excellent organization. A good flow of communication allows all co-workers to feel involved in the vision and partial goals. Implementation and reporting should not be so difficult in this current multi-medium focused society.

Per Gisselsson, one of my most faithful leaders and co-workers always says, "It is the German blood in you that likes order and discipline!" Yeah, well I am no more German than Per is Danish! I am an Austrian! When it comes to this accusation, I'm not sure if it is a low blow or not. All kidding aside, I believe that it is the Spirit of God in me that loves order, discipline, harmony and peace! I have good administrators, real professionals like Martina Almqvist, Sven-Inge Widell, Andreas Gustafsson and Stephanie Elvelyck. Without all of you, it would not work half as well as it does today!

Chapter 10

OBEY AND RELEASE THE GRACE OF GOD

Throughout David's youth he had an ability to release God's grace over his life by always doing what was right, doing what was pleasing to God. When David wrote his worship songs as a shepherd boy in the desert, God's hand was mightily upon him. When David played in King Saul's court, the anointing of the Spirit of God was upon him. His music was soothing and brought healing, but was also innocently provoking due to his purity before God. David loved God and wanted to do His will as a musician, warrior and later as king. David wanted to serve God's plans and purposes for his time, generation and his people. One of the Christian church's patriarch martyrs, Stephen, says of David:

"...who enjoyed God's favor"

Acts 7:46a

When the Apostle Paul preaches in Antioch in Pisidian he quotes the Prophet Samuel's words from God to King Saul and says of David:

> *"I have found David son of Jesse a man after my own heart; he will do everything I want him to do."*
>
> **Acts 13:22b**

When the young David went out into battle against the Philistine giant Goliath, God's grace rested upon him. Everyone saw it, you could not miss it. King Saul said to his commander Abner:

> *"...whose son is that young man?"*
>
> **1 Samuel 17:55b**

Abner answered, completely blown away by David's bravery, his mouth hanging open, not taking his eyes off David for a second:

> *"As surely as you live, O king, I don't know."*
>
> **1 Samuel 17:55b**

All of Israel saw the grace that rested upon David's life. Grace and anointing makes us look better than we actually are. Grace is like a cloak that God covers us in and like an invisible but nevertheless visible crown on our heads. Grace is a shield from God.

*"You surround them with your favor as with a
shield."*

Psalm 5:12b

Before David had to flee because of Saul's jealousy, he was placed over King Saul's army for a short time. This is what scripture said of him:

*"…this pleased all the people, and Saul's officers as
well."*

1 Samuel 18:5b

Grace rested so strongly over David that Saul had panic and anxiety attacks and began acting irrationally.

When David then had become king over Israel, he continued to do what was right and release the grace of God. When David received the message of King Saul's death, the messenger thought that he had come with good news. But when he reported that he had helped give Saul the final mortal blow, David had his men execute him. David mourned the death of Saul and Jonathan, tore his clothes, fasted and wept loudly.

To love your enemies in the way David did releases God's grace over both the leader and those he leads. David did not depend upon his own strength and experience, but on the grace of God. It clearly proved to be so when he came into battle against the Philistines, especially one specific time.

David was already known as a very experienced and skillful warrior, but he waited in ambush with his mighty men and warriors in a wooded area because God had instructed him to in prayer. David wanted to be sensitive to the voice of God and His instructions before every battle. He refused to rely on routine. David held back his men from attacking and waited for the sound of angels marching in the balsam trees, the signal that the Lord had gone out before them. When the steps of the marching angels were heard, his men went out and had victory in battle. Victory was given to him because he listened, obeyed and released God's grace (2 Samuel 5:22-25).

Sometimes God says things to leaders and when we obey, God's grace comes like a flood. God says to me many times to give things away. It could be a car, a large sum of money, books or clothes. When I obey without hesitation and arguing the grace of God comes over my life. Sometimes He says, say you are sorry, send flowers or invite them to lunch or even a vacation.

When God says something to a leader it is of great importance to many that he obeys. It is then that the grace of God comes down from heaven. Obey quickly and you will release the grace of God over the people you lead!

Queen Esther, in the Persian Empire's great era, obeyed God and a great grace rested over her life.

> *"When he saw Queen Esther standing in the court,*
> *he was pleased with her and held out to her the gold*
> *scepter that was in his hand. So Esther approached*
> *and touched the tip of the scepter. Then the king*
> *asked, "What is it, Queen Esther? What is your*

request? Even up to half the kingdom, it will be given you."

Esther 5:2.3

In the early church in Jerusalem, the first Christians knew how to live in a constant flow of grace. The disciples and apostles knew what keys unlocked the storehouses of God and had access to His enormous supply. Listen and read:

"All the believers were one in heart and mind. No one claimed that any of his possession was his own, but they shared everything they had. With great power the apostles continued to testify to the resurrection of the Lord Jesus, and much grace was upon them all."

Acts 4:32-33

The early church knew exactly how to release grace, power and favor from the God of heaven over the church - strong unity, solidarity, generosity, unselfishness and powerful testimonies.

Chapter 11

HONOR AND PROTECT YOUR ENEMIES

David was, as already mentioned, severely persecuted by his predecessor King Saul and had many opportunities to practice this chapter's title. Several times the young warrior David and his mighty men had opportunities to kill King Saul, but didn't. David refused to take vengeance into his own hands, defend himself or snatch the kingdom. Instead, David waited for God to give Israel and the people to him.

When David lived in En Gedi's mountain fortress, Saul came after him with three thousand soldiers. David hid with his men far back in a cave where King Saul would later chose to relieve himself. David was strongly encouraged by his men to kill Saul, given such a golden opportunity. David crawled on his stomach to the place where the grunting and groaning king was and secretly cut off a piece of his cloak, sparing his life. When Saul had wiped himself and emerged from the cave, David came out into the light and called out to the king with his face bowed to the ground:

"See, my father, look at this piece of your robe in my hand!"

1 Samuel 24:11

David proved to Saul, his soldiers and his own men that he did not wish the king any harm or intend to take justice into his own hands. David left both vengeance and judgment to God, whom he believed in with his whole heart. Saul started crying and in a short moment of spiritual revelation realized his own degraded spiritual state and the fact that David was more righteous than he.

Saul and David meet again when Saul camped out in the Desert of Ziph on the hill of Hakilah. King Saul was lying asleep next to his commanding officer Abner with the army encamped around him. David and Abishai, one of David's mighty men, snuck into their camp at night. They made their way to the sleeping king, without being noticed. As they were standing there over the snoring King, Abishai whispers to David and asks for permission to pierce Saul with his own spear while the King sleeps. David firmly says no and instead takes Saul's spear that was thrust into the ground and his water jug that was by his head.

When David and Abishai came out of the camp, they stood on top of the hill some distance away. They called out to Abner and wondered why he had not sufficiently protected his king during the night. David instructed them to look for the king's spear and water jug that had been placed just above the king's pillow. Abner and Saul's soldiers were shamed. Saul started to cry as once again he realized David's greatness. David refused to, as he himself expressed it:

"...I would not lay a hand on the Lord's anointed."
1 Samuel 26:23b

When King Saul was killed, David mourned. He fasted, cried and wrote a song in memory of King Saul. The song is remembered in history as lament of the bow (2 Samuel 1:18). After Saul's death war broke out between the house of Saul and the house of David. Saul's chief commander of the army, Abner, decided after a while to seek out David, make a covenant with him and encourage all of Israel to stand behind and support David as their king. Abner thought that the time had come when they should finally crown David king over all of the tribes of Israel. David received Abner, was willing to make peace with him and organized a party for him and his followers. Joab, David's commander of the army, did not like David's peace treaty. Abner had killed Joab's brother, Asael during a previous battle. Joab sent for Abner and murdered him. David again showed his righteousness and greatness when he heard about the murder of Abner:

"Then David said to Joab and all the people with him "tear your clothes and put on sackcloth and walk in mourning in front of Abner". King David himself walked behind the bier. They buried Abner

in Hebron, and the king wept aloud at Abner's tomb.
All the people wept also. The king sang this lament
for Abner: "should Abner have died as the lawless
die?"

2 Samuel 3:31-33

"Then the king said to his men, "Do you not realize
that a prince and a great man has fallen in Israel
today?"

2 Samuel 3:38

King David even mourned the death of his enemies.
David honored and protected all of his enemies and trusted
in God as his defender.

This is not easy to do, I know this from personal experience and I have not always succeeded at practicing this. It's
good to know that there is forgiveness with God through
Jesus Christ. This principle of leadership is very much based
on Biblical principles. Jesus said in his famous sermon on
the mount:

"Love your enemies and pray for those who
persecute you."

Matthew 5:44

Dear reader, be careful of discussions and argumentative
situations that just want to entice you into endless debates.
Debates, which eventually rob your heart of its purity, leave
you sad, hurt and bitter. I made a decision a few years ago

that I would not take part in Christian panel debates or be part of discussions in Christian newspapers or on Christian homepages. After a personal crisis and a long time of self examination, deep repentance from bitterness and strife in Sweden, I finally said: "Never again." I will willingly stand up for the truth and the Word of God and fight for Christian values in secular media or the political sphere. But I will not be involved in the internal Christian sandbox of futile debate.

Lord Jesus, forgive me that I ever stooped so low into the sandbox of Christian politics. Keep all of my dear Christian colleagues from mud-slinging and church politics' different cliques and conflicts. Lord, help us all! For me, this has meant sending many bouquets of flowers and letters to all of my Christian friends to finally appease my conscience and get some peace on the inside. The Spirit of the Lord loves temperance, forbearing, love and honesty.

What makes a leader truly great is usually shown in the amount of self-control he displays when he is attacked or questioned in his leadership or for how he leads. A great leader does not defend himself, his reputation or name, but leaves that battle to the Lord and to his covenant friends. A great leader honors and protects even his enemies. God help us all to dare to live this out in our lives!

One time a journalist called me from one of our so called Christian newspapers in Sweden. He wanted to know all of the dirty details about another Swedish evangelist's failure and fall. The journalist knew that I had a lot of information concerning this. When I cut off the conversation with a sharp, "No comment", the journalist became very angry. "Hasn't he hurt you too, Johannes?" he asked. "Yes, of course," I answered, "I have cried many a tear. I think that this whole situation is a tragedy." "Yeah, but…" the journalist continued to say, "help me to expose him then!"

No, why should we get messed up in Christian fleshly gossip and gorge on other's mistakes and failures? Instead, honor and protect your enemies, and those who have disappointed you.

Chapter 12

THE ART OF
SIMPLICITY

King David succeeded at the art of being very organized, disciplined and excellent, without becoming exclusive and snobbish. Sure, King David had some difficult times in his forty year reign, not to mention his affair with Bathsheba, the wife of Uriah as told in 2 Samuel, Chapter 11. Sure, his prosperity had gone to his head in connection with the census he took of the people during the last part of his reign as King (2 Samuel, Chapter 24) and through his sin he brought on a plague over Israel, through which seventy-thousand of his people died. Despite this, David had the quality and practiced the art of simplicity during most of his life and in all of his great successes.

David was very aware of his simple background as a shepherd boy and most likely often reminded himself of where he came from. David was popular with the people as any great leader must be and able to live in two worlds at

the same time. David made decisions that had great consequences for the whole nation and at the same time he could
identify with the average, everyday person in the country
side as well as on the streets of Jerusalem. He had a way
of speaking, style and tone that was met with respect in
different levels of society and knew exactly when he should
be King and when he should be friend. David had a sense of
humor, was musical and a gifted speaker. David knew that
he would not lose his respect and authority by mixing on a
social level with his soldiers and servants. David won their
hearts and was liked by almost everyone. Most thought that
in some way they knew the king personally, even though it
was impossible in reality.

When the Ark of the Covenant was brought into Jerusalem
there was great celebration with dancing, singing and joy in
the streets. It says of David:

"David, wearing a linen, danced before the Lord
with all his might,"

2 Samuel 6:14

David danced his heart out. The sweat ran down his face,
he was totally free from prestige and what others thought of
him. The dignity that the Spirit of God gives us is something
totally different than worldly pride and prestige. David
pulled out all the stops, quite lightly clothed too, I might
add. He danced together with the people of Israel before their
great God with joy that the Ark was brought into Jerusalem.
It continues to say:

*"As the ark of the Lord was entering the City of
David, Michal daughter of Saul watched from a
window. And when she saw King David leaping
and dancing before the Lord, she despised him in her
heart."*

2 Samuel 6:16

When David came home that night, his wife Michal re-
proached him saying that he had behaved without dignity
and also exposed himself to the slave girls. She spewed out
her disdain and contempt over the joyful dance he had made
earlier that day. David answered her and said:

*"David said to Michal, It was before the Lord, who
chose me rather than your father or anyone from his
house when he appointed me ruler over the Lord's
people Israel – I will celebrate before the Lord. I will
become even more undignified than this, and I will
be humiliated in my own eyes. But by these slave
girls you spoke of, I will be held in honor."*

2 Samuel 6:21-22

Michal, the daughter of Saul, had no children and was
barren for as long as she lived. Pride, prestige and snobbish
attitudes usually lead to spiritual sterility and unfruitful-
ness.

I want to dance, sing, preach and shout out my love to
Jesus, no matter what anyone thinks! I want to be a leader for
a spiritually fertile and life-giving people, not an exclusive,

religious cemetery with a following of morticians and dead fish. Jesus was a friend of prostitutes and publicans, tax authorities for the Roman government. He socialized with those who were society's greatest outcasts and was not ashamed of it.

I love to socialize with non-Christians and some of my greatest friends are atheists and Hindus. I like to be in the company of our church members, missionaries, Bible school students and the new converts. I have never lost anything as a leader because I have laughed, hugged, teased and social-ized a lot with people, quite the opposite!

Chapter 13

CHARACTER, INTEGRITY AND EXCELLENCE

The God of the Bible is good, generous, merciful and kind. The God of David was not a slave driver, but a wonderful father and the great Shepherd of Israel. When a leader experiences great success they can sometimes forget who gave them growth. They are tempted to believe that it was their own capacity and ability that has built and gathered the ones they lead. They are gripped with fear, panic and a feeling of inadequacy. They desperately try to do things in their own strength. The leader is chased by the success he has made and it becomes a prison. He starts to desperately long for freedom and a way out of the rat-race. He starts dreaming about starting to work as a travel guide in a Singapore or Thailand tourist office! Are you describing yourself now Johannes? Yes, of course! For a short moment when I am tempted to believe that I alone carry the responsibility for Mission SOS, SOS Mission Bible College and Europe's whole Pentecostal movement, I start dreaming of fleeing to the Southeast Asian Islands.

Even if they all started out right, success, greatness, influence and successful leadership has gone to too many a great leaders' head. To start well is important, but to finish well is even more important. To finish with your flag still waving at the top is a good goal for every leader. In light of this, you must understand why we need to teach about integrity and character when we strive and stretch for large Christian churches, organizations and companies.

When David had sinned with the young married woman Bathsheba and had killed her husband, the prophet Nathan came with a message from God:

> *"This is what the Lord, the God of Israel, says: I anointed you king over Israel, and I delivered you from the hand of Saul. I gave your master's house to you, and gave you the house of Israel and Judah. And if all this had been too little, I would have given you even more."*
>
> **2 Samuel 12:7b-8**

We can learn so much from just these one and a half verses about God's nature and his love for David:

1. God gives leadership, security, wealth, happiness and influence

2. God is generous and does not withhold any of his goodness
3. God mourns David's lack of integrity

This means we always need to be brutally honest with ourselves, unpretentious and humble. We need to be able to ask for forgiveness if we are to survive as a leader.

Qualifications of a Leader

This chapter's teaching is targeted more towards church leaders than business leaders.

Many ask me if one can be disqualified for leadership even if you have most of the qualities and characteristics of a leader. Yes, absolutely. The Bible is very clear on this, especially those who are in New Testament church leadership. They were first to be tested and tried. They were to live up to a certain standard and have high moral character. They were to be mature before they were appointed and could take over in their role as pastor or church leader.

In his letter to his spiritual sons Timothy and Titus, the Apostle Paul clearly lists these qualifications for leadership in his instructions concerning the appointing and dedication of leaders. We will study two passages of scripture in the New Testament and the pastoral letters together:

According to 1 Timothy 3:1-13 and Titus 1:5-11, a summary of Paul's leadership qualifications would look like something like this:

1. There are no major accusations against the leader
2. Husband of one wife and being faithful in marriage
3. Children who are believers and not rebellious
4. Prioritize their family first
5. Respected and not a know it all
6. Has a hospitable and open home
7. A learned and good teacher
8. Does not abuse alcohol
9. Self-controlled and does not have outbursts of anger
10. Generous, not stingy or loves money
11. Dependable and keeps his promises
12. A sound and balanced teaching
13. Kind-hearted and encouraging
14. Mature in the faith and not a new believer
15. Has a good reputation among non-believers
16. Someone who has the courage to silence gossipers and trouble-makers by countering their attack if needed

Both the head leaders and ministers of help need to first be tested according to the list above. If there is no reason to reproach them, they're appointed and installed into their specific area of leadership (1 Timothy 3:10). Since Paul lists both qualifications and the need to test if they meet the requirements, it was obvious that not everyone was approved, i.e. met the standards of a church leader.

I believe that this does not refer to the believer's life before repentance and salvation. The life you live after salvation is what determines if one qualifies for leadership or not. God forgives and restores everything. However, leadership is not about how God sees you. It is also determined by others. Do they think you are a worthy example and roll model. Will they follow you as a leader? This is what is said about Jesus:

> *"And Jesus grew in wisdom and stature, and in*
> *favor with God and men."*
> **Luke 2:52**

Yes, it is important what people think of me. That those whom I am to lead actually follow when I take a step out in a direction and go forward.

Restoration

The following question would be: Is there restoration for someone who has been a leader, but has failed, and wants to start over again? Yes, I believe so. However, I am not so sure that everyone must, or should make a comeback. There are cases where I believe that one has actually used up all the faith, confidence and believability as a leader. The leader does both he and others a favor by completely refraining from entering into ministry again.

Instead of fighting for the rest of his life to regain his leadership role, which is void of confidence, it is better to do something completely different and enjoy his life in God's wonderful forgiveness and restoration.

Some leaders want to get back into ministry. They feel that they have more to give and even believe that people will once again have confidence in them. This situation depends on the former leader putting himself under mentorship, and being willing to go through a renewed testing of his leadership by a proven leadership, prior to entering a renewed position of authority. I cannot help but say how deeply troubling it is to see how lightly we view leadership-failure-restoration in the western world today.

Divorce

You don't make a comeback just a few weeks after, or even months or a year after being unfaithful or getting a divorce. We are talking about a restoration period of three to five years, at least. A person needs time to heal after a great failure or tragedy. If there were children involved, it can take even longer. A leader is not irreplaceable during a difficult crisis and people will understand.

It is important to point out that a leader is not a leader for their own sake. One is a leader for the sake of others, first and foremost. A leader washes the feet of those he serves and leads by example. Sometimes I hear people say, "But what will he do now? He has nothing else! He can't do anything else!" As it was for their own sake that they became a leader!

I really do not understand that type of reasoning at all. They will have to take a regular job and work hard like everyone else. A former leader needs to work on his life, his broken relationships and build up renewed confidence again. Other leaders determine when the former leader is ready and healed enough for a new task, not the one who has failed.

Sure, we need to be better at restoring leaders that have fallen. We need to sincerely be there for them because they have fallen and hurt themselves. We cannot love and cry enough with those who have wrecked and ruined the possibility of continuing with that which they thought would be their life-long calling and their greatest joy in life!

When it comes to standards, morals and strong character you can never be too clear or too strict. Character is the very foundation for us being able to live a long life all the way to the end. Not three years as a leader, but 30-60 years, yes, even longer if we aim at living until we are 120 and start young!

Tee Totallers

In Mission SOS we have tightened up on our leadership qualifications. We are actually even more radical than the Biblical norm in some areas. You may say, isn't that a bit presumptuous and arrogant, Johannes? I know that the apostle Paul would have liked and given his approval if he had seen what kind of world we work in now, almost two thousand years after he gave the first instructions regarding leadership to Timothy and Titus.

We not only require moderation when it comes to the usage of alcohol in our organization, but total abstinence. We are completely sober and do not accept any kind of alcohol use among our missionaries and co-workers.

But you are an Austrian, Johannes! You are from central Europe; shouldn't you have a more liberal view of alcohol? No, dear friend, do you dare listen to a central European? I have seen the back side of the Austrian wine and beer culture. Drunkenness, physical abuse and unfaithfulness go hand in hand with the spirits in the glass and the devil in the bottle.

We need a new sobriety movement in Europe and especially in Germany, Austria, Switzerland, Italy and France! Not to speak of Eastern Europe and dare I say, America! People drink themselves to death and we need more than ever drug-free environments, places where the newly saved can feel safe and relaxed. The Apostle Paul said:

> *"It is better not to eat meat or drink wine or to do anything else that will cause your brother to fall."*
> **Romans 14:21**

The Christian's duty to love means that I who am strong should refrain from showing my strength out of love and respect for those who are weak. Duty to love, what a beautiful thing!

Integrity

Integrity is a fantastic word! Courage to stand for one's beliefs is a beautiful thing. It means that as a leader you stand for something. As time goes by, even your opponents respect you for it. Who can depend upon a leader that changes his opinions all the time?

We need leaders who have backbone and stand up for what they believe, ones who are not wimpy and wishy-washy. The leader that looks me straight in the eye and says that he does not agree with me usually becomes a really good friend in time. Honesty and frankness is fantastic and completely necessary ingredients in a strong relationship. Who says that we have to totally agree on everything all the time to be able to laugh and spend time with each other? As an evangelist I can get into trouble in this area because I love to spend time with non-Christians. Being in agreement or at least respecting being under authority is very important, especially if we are going to work together closely and intimately, to stand together in the same Christian church, organization or company.

I have an expression that many of my co-workers in Mission SOS have heard many times. When someone asks me, "How are you? How is it going these days?" I usually answer, "Good, thank-you, same vision, same style and the same wife!"

Some people get a little offended because they don't think that is a sound development in my life. They would rather that I would say something like, "Well, you know, not everything is so black and white anymore. Life has taught me that one must compromise and find a way to navigate in deep water." No. Not me. I don't want to play that game!

In some circles the slogan is almost mandatory. New vision, new style and new wife and preferably every year! If you have failed in your life as a leader, don't get angry with me now. I love you, dear friend. You can make a comeback! But please let your difficult experiences teach us all how important integrity and character really are, so that you don't trip and fall again. Help me, you who has had this tragic experience, to sharpen and instill this in leaders all around the world!

Excellence

"Do you see a man skilled in his work? He will serve before kings; he will not serve before obscure men."
Proverbs 22:29

Excellence is to take what you have and make the best of it. It doesn't necessarily always have to be expensive. Excellence is not primarily about nice clothes, cars and the latest technical equipment in the church, organization or company. If the economic resources are available, then naturally we can choose the best and focus on quality as long as it is righteous and possible. But excellence is mostly about stewardship and sticking to the budget. Excellence comes from the inside not the outside.

I have met excellent leaders outside of churches that are made of corrugated metal; leaders who only own one pair of shoes. Excellence is showing every receipt, to keep the books, paying the bills and taxes on time. Excellence is also accountability, authorized auditors and to not putting oneself in unnecessary debt, but instead have buildings as collateral and much more.

Excellence is about being able to admit that I can't do everything, daring to ask for help when there are people with expertise and competence that I don't have. Excellence is beautiful.

Maria and I have been through everything, feels like it anyway, even if it is far from true. Sometimes a large church will put us up in a luxury hotel and spoil us and give us fantastic remuneration for our ministry. Other times, we sleep at the airport and do not receive payment at all. We are always happy anyway! We join with the Apostle Paul when he says:

> *"I am not saying this because I am in need, for I have learned to be content whatever the circumstances. I know what it is to be in need, and I know what it is to have plenty. I have learned the secret of being content in any and every situation, whether well fed or hungry, whether living in plenty or in want. I can do everything through him who gives me strength."*
> **Philippians 4:11-13**

The Amritzer family is simply missionaries, no more, no less. We love the life God has given us! Once we came as a whole family to a small church in Sweden. The whole family was to stay in the church's guestroom. Maria still speaks of that guestroom. It was so simple and small, but excellent! What? How? Well, it was clean, not a speck of dust to be seen. The beds were nicely made and someone had put some chocolate candies on our pillows, just like a fancy hotel would do. The towels lying on the bed were new. There was a little bowl on the table with fruit, candy, and some soda bottles, including the bottle opener! There was a small welcome card with some nice things written to us.

We still wonder who did all that. We felt so welcome! The church only had approximately 100 members, but they spoiled us with pizza for the whole family after the first meeting, and then paid us much more than they could afford to after the weekend services were over. We will never forget that church as long as we live. Everything they did exuded excellence. Excellence is to be thorough in the personal appreciation you want to give, or in the task that has been given you.

In Norway, a church contacted my secretary and asked how old my children were, what their names were and what their interests were. In the hotel room, there were special presents for Alicia and Adam. They had also organized several fun activities for the sake of the kids while I was teaching and preaching. Admittedly, they were one of Norway's largest churches, but the Amritzer family will never forget that week or the love that they showed to us. My children's favorite country on earth for a very long time was Norway.

Hospitality

A warm and open home is a leader's strongest forum in both the training of disciples and the raising up of those whom he is leading. Around the kitchen table, the couch or in the yard with a cup of coffee in hand is usually the best form of coaching leaders.

Prayer, Bible reading, conversations, dinners, games and fun around the kitchen table usually has a longer influence than the most professional lectures with power point and multi-media presentations in a conference room. It is even easier to open up, cry and share together in the relaxed environment of a leader's home.

At Mission SOS and SOS Mission Bible College we put a lot of emphasis on open, safe and cozy homes. Almost all of our leaders have people living with them or staying in their guest rooms. Extra mouths and stomachs to feed for breakfast or dinner is commonplace in the Amritzer family's home and we have always had people living with us. A warm open home is probably the closest thing to early Christian fellowship that we can find in our otherwise high-tech and stressful society.

Finally

My prayer for what I have written here in these simple teachings is that leaders would receive help from the Holy Spirit to be better and continue to develop. Visionary leaders need Godly character if their faith goals are going to be more than just cool slogans. Even if leadership structures, rolls and titles are completely necessary, integrity is even more important in the long run. I hope that you have received a blessing and have been enriched in your life calling and task. God give us a strong spiritual leadership in Sweden and around the world!

About the Author

Johannes Amritzer is a powerful evangelist and Bible teacher who has traveled around the world for 17 years. He preaches the Gospel, mostly among people groups who have never before heard of Jesus Christ. Johannes and his wife Maria started Evangelical Mission SOS International in 1996. During their ministry they have seen tens of thousands of people receive Jesus as their Savior, healed in their bodies, baptized in the Holy Spirit and delivered from evil spirits. Mission SOS has its headquarters in Stockholm Sweden.

Other Books and Pamphlets by the Author:

- How Jesus Healed the Sick (and how you can too!)
- Baptized in Holy Spirit and Fire
- A New Missions Wave
- Practical Discipleship Training School
- Saved in the Last Days

For more information about Mission SOS or to order materials contact us at:
www.missionsos.com
usoffice@missionsos.org
Telephone: +1 (412) 487 7220